MW01154685

SPORTS BIOGRAPHIES

SIMONE BILES

KENNY ABDO

USA

Fly!
An Imprint of Abdo Zoom
abdobooks.com

abdobooks.com

Published by Abdo Zoom, a division of ABDO, P.O. Box 398166, Minneapolis, Minnesota 55439. Copyright © 2021 by Abdo Consulting Group, Inc. International copyrights reserved in all countries. No part of this book may be reproduced in any form without written permission from the publisher. Fly!™ is a trademark and logo of Abdo Zoom.

Printed in the United States of America, North Mankato, Minnesota.
052020
092020

Photo Credits: AP Images, Alamy, Icon Sportswire, iStock, newscom, Shutterstock
Production Contributors: Kenny Abdo, Jennie Forsberg, Grace Hansen
Design Contributors: Dorothy Toth, Neil Klinepier

Library of Congress Control Number: 2019956163

Publisher's Cataloging-in-Publication Data

Names: Abdo, Kenny, author.
Title: Simone Biles / by Kenny Abdo
Description: Minneapolis, Minnesota : Abdo Zoom, 2021 | Series: Sports biographies | Includes online resources and index.
Identifiers: ISBN 9781098221416 (lib. bdg.) | ISBN 9781098222390 (ebook) | ISBN 9781098222888 (Read-to-Me ebook)
Subjects: LCSH: Biles, Simone, 1997---Juvenile literature. | Professional athletes-United States--Biography--Juvenile literature. | Women gymnasts--Biography-Juvenile literature. | Olympic athletes-Biography--Juvenile literature.
Classification: DDC 796.44092 [B]--dc23

TABLE OF CONTENTS

SIMONE BILES

With total command, Simone Biles has won more World **Championship** gold medals in gymnastics than anyone else in history.

The young gymnast is one of the most respected athletes in the sport. Biles has gained popularity and earned records around the world.

EARLY YEARS

Simone Biles was born in Columbus, Ohio, in 1997. In 2003, she and her sister, Adria, were **adopted** by their grandparents.

Biles won the gold at the 2014 US Classic. She wowed the crowd when she **debuted** her trademark move, the double-flip with half twist.

In July 2015, Biles announced she was going pro. That same year she took home four gold medals at the World **Championships** in Glasgow, Scotland. The next season would take her to her first **Olympics** in Rio de Janeiro, Brazil!

At the 2016 **Olympics**, the US women's gymnastics team took home gold for the third time in history. Biles won three individual golds and a bronze!

Biles kept on gathering golds. She swept all of her events at the 2018 US Gymnastics **Championships**. In 2019, Biles earned her fifth **all-around** gold at the World Championships.

19

LEGACY

Before the 2020 season, Biles had the most World **Championship** gymnast medals, with an impressive collection of 25. She also had 19 gold World Champ medals, another record-winning number!

WORLD CHAMPIONSHIPS
ARTISTIC GYMNASTICS
STUTTGART 2019

Biles works with the Mattress Firm Foster Kids program to support **foster** families around the United States. The foundation has donated thousands of items, including clothes and school supplies, to foster homes.

GLOSSARY

adopted – legally made the son or daughter of someone who is not a biological parent.

all-around – a category of gymnastics that includes all of the events. The all-around champion of an event earns the highest total score from all events combined.

championship – a game held to find a first-place winner.

debut – a first appearance.

foster – giving or receiving care in a family not related by birth or adoption.

Olympic games – the biggest sporting event in the world that is divided into summer and winter games.

title – a first-place position in a contest.

ONLINE RESOURCES

Booklinks
NONFICTION NETWORK
FREE! ONLINE NONFICTION RESOURCES

To learn more about
Simone Biles, please visit
abdobooklinks.com or scan
this QR code. These links
are routinely monitored
and updated to provide the
most current information
available.

INDEX